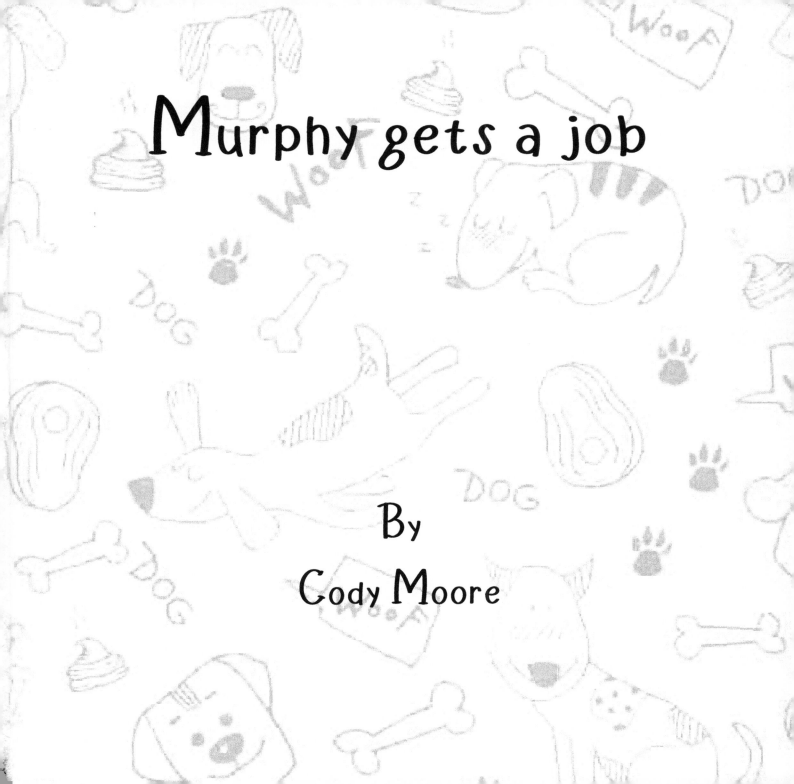

Murphy gets a job

By

Cody Moore

Dedication

I would like to dedicate this book to several groups. First I have to give thanks and praise to God. Second, to my incredible family, who often shoulder the burden of the dedication needed to attend training and fundraising events. It does not go unnoticed and I could not do any of this without your support. Third, to my fire department family that has always been supportive of us and this program. Fourth, to those who serve alongside us on search and rescue teams. You are all truly men and women with servants hearts. And last but not least. Thank you to everyone reading this book. Our program is only successful because of the support you have all shown us. Thank you so much! To learn more about our program please go to www.idahodisasterdogs.com

My name is Murphy. I am a yellow Labrador. This is the story of how I became a working dog. I remember it like it was yesterday. It all started when I was a puppy... it was a great day.

When I was a puppy, I was adopted. The man who adopted me said, "Murphy, you look like a smart pup. Would you like a job as a search and rescue dog? If someone gets lost, hurt, or trapped, you will use your nose to find them." I liked the sound of that. This was going to be a fun adventure.

The man told me that he would be my person, and I would be his pup. He told me that I was going to go live with him. That we were going to work hard but we would have a lot of fun too. I had a good feeling about this.

My person was the best. When we got to his house, he gave me a bunch of new stuff. I got a new bed, a new leash, and new toys. I also got a working dog "In Training" collar. I couldn't imagine a better life. I get to live with my person and have all this fun stuff. I think this makes us family.

The best news was that my brother Duke was also adopted. He was going to become a search and rescue pup too. He would live with a different person, but I would get to see him when I went to work. Duke is a smart pup too. I know we will grow into great working dogs.

Our first day training with the search and rescue team was inspiring. They gave us our very own Search Dog vests. They were a little big, but they said that we would grow into them. I can only imagine how silly I looked with that big vest on, but I felt so proud to be wearing it.

The older dogs were really nice too. They told us that we have to learn a lot if we want to be search and rescue pups. People will be counting on us. There is no higher calling for a dog than to be a working dog.

My person and I were always together. Wherever he went, I went with him. He works at the fire station, which means now I do too. All of the other firefighters quickly became my new friends. We loved to work and play together. I enjoy being a part of this team.

On one of my first days at the fire station, I dug in the trash and accidentally made a big mess. This did not make my new firefighter friends happy. I know now, that getting in the trash is not a good thing to do. I felt sorry and knew I still had a lot to learn. Learning lessons can be hard, but it is important to always be learning.

Working with the firefighters was a good example for me. They are passionate about helping people. They are constantly training and learning. It's exciting to be at the station. One minute we are training, and then suddenly, the fire station bell rings. Everyone races to the fire engine, and off it goes to help someone. I hope to be as dedicated as them.

Every day my person and I trained together. He taught me many new things. We always called it work, but most of the time, it was just plain fun. At the end of the training, he always said, "Murphy, you're a good boy." If we kept working hard, then soon I would be a working dog.

First, I had to learn to listen. He called it obedience. I learned how to come when called. How to walk right next to him. I learned to lie down and stay. I never understood how laying down was work, but he gave me treats every time I stayed put. Then he would say, "Good boy Murphy." He called the treats my paycheck. No matter what you call it, treats are a great reward!

Next, he taught me how to run in the direction he was pointing. Each time I did it, he would reward me with a game of fetch and say, "Good boy Murphy." I never get sick of being praised or playing fetch. Chasing a ball is one of the greatest games, and it's great exercise.

After I learned obedience, he taught me how to find people. He kept calling it search, but it seemed like we were playing hide and seek. Can you believe I get to play hide and seek for work? There is nothing I like more than searching for people.

The more we practiced, the better I became. My nose became so strong I could find my friends wherever they were hiding. Especially if they forgot to shower.... Pew wee. They told me I had a super sniffer. A super sniffer makes a great search pup.

Once I got a little older, my person started teaching me agility. I learned to walk through dark tunnels and how to climb ladders. It was scary at first, but my person kept me safe every step of the way.

Then I learned how to walk on wobbly surfaces and across a teeter totter. Eventually, I was able to do it all on my own, and he said, "Good boy Murphy." Overcoming your fears is a great way to grow.

Some days I get to go see my friend Doc, the veterinarian. She always tells me that it is important to stay healthy. That way, I can do my job when someone needs help. She works hard to be good at her job so that I can be good at mine. If I get hurt, she patches me up. If I don't feel good, she makes me better. Doc is truly one of the greats!

I will let you in on a secret. There is another reason Doc is so great. Doc likes to keep dog treats all over her clinic. There is always a jar of treats within reach. Many of Doc's friends work at the clinic. Whenever one of them walks by, I try to act cute and show them my puppy eyes. I call it "acting labrador-able." If I can get their attention, they usually give me a treat. Treats come in so many wonderful flavors.

Before I knew it, the time had come. It was time to take the search and rescue tests. Was I nervous? Of course, but this is what I had been training for. I would need to pass two tests that determined if I was ready. Getting the chance to go take the tests was a great opportunity.

I wasn't quite two years old yet, but I had been working towards this since I was two months old. We spent many months preparing for this moment. I was ready. I knew I could do it. Everyone on my team played a part in getting me ready for these tests. It is important to remember those who have helped you, I owe them all a BIG THANK YOU!

To get to the test, we first had to travel. We went on a long car ride to the testing site. When we arrived, Duke and I lined up with all the other dogs. All of us were ready to show how hard we had worked and how much we wanted to be search and rescue pups. It was sure to be a challenge.

The first test encompassed everything we had been working on. Obedience, agility, and search. It was a long and exhausting day. I did everything exactly how I practiced. I listened well, traversed the agility course, and found the hidden people. Afterward, my person said, "Good boy Murphy!" Now we wait for the results. Waiting for results is a great way to practice patience.

At the end of the day, they announced every dog that passed. I waited patiently, and then finally, they said, "Good boy Murphy, you passed." YES! I was halfway there. Hard work pays off. Passing the first test was a big accomplishment.

The next test was far away. I put on my search dog vest, and we got on an airplane. We traveled all day, and what a journey it was. The lady that sat next to me gave me lots of pets during the flight. The pilot told me that I did a good job on the flight. He also told me that I earned my wings that day. Airplane rides are pretty neat too.

Eventually, we made it to the final test. One final exercise to prove I am ready to be a search and rescue dog. The final test was a big search to see if I could find all the hiding people. Ready, set, Go Search! I searched hard. Some of those people were great hiders. But remember, I have a great super sniffer.

First, one person, then the next. Before I knew it, I had found them all! The evaluators said, "Good boy Murphy." I couldn't believe it, I PASSED! I was now a certified search and rescue pup! Guess what else? Duke passed both of his tests too! What a great achievement.

My person told me, "Great job Murphy, you truly are the best boy." Then he told me that we had just one thing left, a final surprise. In honor of me passing the final test, he took me out for my first cheeseburger! What a treat! Cheeseburgers are so yummy! But the best part was sharing a meal with my person.

At the next search and rescue training, the team awarded me with my own working dog collar. It's official. I have a job. I joined the ranks of the dogs that had always inspired me. Now the real work begins. I was no longer a working dog in training. I was now Murphy, the Search, and Rescue Pup... and that was a great day!

Donation Page

Running a canine search and rescue team requires countless hours of training. Every member of our team volunteers their time to support our mission. Along with the time involved comes the unfortunate aspect of expenses. Not only bringing new canines into our program, but also keeping them healthy, trained and ready for duty is a tremendous expense. We have a few amazing sponsors who have helped to offset this cost. Today more than ever, it still requires additional fundraising. By purchasing this book you have taken a part in supporting our cause, and we can't thank you enough. If you would like to learn more about our team, make a donation, or see pictures from our team, you can find us online at www.idahodisasterdogs.com. We appreciate your continued support of our mission. We do this for all of you, but equally importantly, we can't do this without you.

 Website

 Donate Page

 Facebook

 Instagram

FAQ:

Is Murphy a real USAR Canine? Yes Murphy is a USAR Canine. He has been a real good boy!

Do dogs really go the fire station? The dogs do come to work with us. This is invaluable for their training. They do not respond to normal 911 calls for service with us, but they do reside at the firehouse while their handler is on duty.

How long does it take to train a dog? Typically the process to be test ready, takes 1-2 years. The dogs are not eligible to test until they are at least 18 months old.

Which breed of dogs? There is no defined breed of dog that is required. However, you will often see retrievers, shepherds, pointers, etc.

How to get involved? There are many ways to be involved in SAR. By purchasing this book, you have already supported our team. All donations are needed, and much appreciated. If you would like to be more involved we encourage you to research the different disciplines of SAR, and then contact a team near you.

Is it hard to train a dog? To train a dog to be a working dog takes a lot of time and energy. It is a challenge, but it's worth it.

Are dogs needed? With all of the technology today, it is a fair question, are dogs still needed? The answer is a resounding yes. Their natural ability is still significantly faster than our modern technology. A well trained dog is not only reliable but fast.

Where can I learn more? Head on over to www.idahodisasterdogs.com

 Website   Donate Page

 Facebook   Instagram

Terms:

Search and Rescue: The search for and provision of aid to people who are in distress or danger. Often someone who is lost, trapped, injured, etc. Also abbreviated SAR

Type of Search and Rescue: There are many types of SAR including, Urban Search and Rescue (USAR), Wilderness or Ground SAR, Mountain Rescue, Maritime SAR, Combat SAR, and more.

Urban Search and Rescue: Urban Search and Rescue is a type of search and rescue. This type of SAR has an emphasis on collapsed buildings and similar events. Events often caused by earthquakes, terrorism, extreme weather, etc. The handler and canine receive specialized training to work in this environment. The mission of USAR is to locate, extricate and medically stabilize. *This is the type of SAR that Canine Murphy is involved in.*

Teams: Although this book is about Murphy's journey to become certified; it is important to acknowledge that canine search is a small component of the entire rescue team. Every position is essential to successful completion of the mission. These teams are often called a Task Force.

Canine: Canine means, of relating to, or resembling a dog. Canine is used often to reference working/service dogs. Canine is also abbreviated K9.

Search and Rescue Canine: A canine that is specially trained to function within a search and rescue team, to locate lost, trapped, injured or otherwise missing people.

Search: Search is the process of looking for the missing person. In canine search, the dog is using their nose to locate the scent of the missing person or people.

Alert: An alert is the trained behavior a canine uses to notify their handler that they have located what they were searching for. In the case of SAR, they have located the person. In USAR, they often can smell the person, but are unable to see them, due to the event (such as a building collapse).

Obedience: At the foundational level this is about keeping the dog safe. It builds into the dog learning their boundaries and then how to work alongside their handlers and other people/dogs. It also gets the dog to respond to requests from their handlers.

Agility: This is a training element to teach the dog how to control their body and navigate difficult obstacles. In the sporting world, this is often used for competition. For the SAR world, this teaches the canine how to be safe on unfamiliar terrain, as well as how to get to other areas that would otherwise be inaccessible.

Dog Team: One handler and one dog.

The Collar: The SAR world does not have a specific "in training" or "working dog" collar. Our team awards a canine with a special collar, after completion of their training and testing process.

Canine Vest: Service and Working Dogs are typically identified by the vest they wear. The vest usually has their name and job on it. Many canines wear these vests while working. USAR is different.

When searching they do not wear their vest or collar due to safety concerns.

Testing: All of the canines are trained and tested to a strict standard. Due to the nature of their work, the dog team (see above) must prove that they are competent. Testing is stressful and challenging.

Rewards: The rewards are truly the dogs paycheck. We believe the reward needs to be worth the work done, to encourage the dog to continue working. This reward is usually treats and/or play (Ex. Game of tug of war). The cheeseburger referenced in this book, is a special treat awarded to Murphy after successful completion of each test. This is not a normal reward, but just a special time Murphy and his handler share.

About the Author and Murphy

Cody Moore is a firefighter paramedic with the Coeur d'Alene Fire Department, in North Idaho. Coeur d'Alene Fire proudly operates Idaho Task Force 1, a state Urban Search and Rescue Team. Part of that team consists of a canine program. Cody is a program coordinator for the canine division as well as a canine Handler. Cody and Murphy are also members of FEMA Washington Task Force 1. Murphy is a real working dog, and all of his stories are based off of real events. Murphy truly got a cheeseburger after his first test. He truly earned his wings on his first flight. Murphy and Cody began working together in 2013, when Murphy was seven weeks old. Through their time together they have been able to serve on the local, state and federal level. If you would like to learn more please head to

www.idahodisasterdogs.com

 Website

 Donate Page

 Facebook

 Instagram